Angie,
the Tundra Swan

A True Story

BY TODD DANIEL PILGRIM

WITH ILLUSTRATIONS BY JULIANN FRASER

This book is dedicated to my two children,
THOR AND SHANTELLE PILGRIM.

One day I went for a short drive in the forest and then hiked to one of my favourite places.
On the way back from my hike, I saw a swan sitting alongside the road. I said to myself,
"HOW UNUSUAL TO SEE A SWAN BY THE ROAD."

I started walking up to the swan to take a closer look. Its feathers were mostly silvery gray, and it had a pinkish bill with a black tip. This told me that *THE SWAN WAS YOUNG* and had not fully matured into an adult swan.

As I got closer to the swan, it didn't try to fly away. Instead, it started walking down the highway, and I noticed its left wing was drooping. It was as I expected: *THE SWAN WAS INJURED.*

I was afraid that a car might run over the swan or that a fox or wolf might catch it for dinner, so **_EVER SO GENTLY_** I picked it up and put it in the passenger seat of my truck.

At first, the swan was a little scared of her unfamiliar surroundings as she began squawking very loudly. I guess she probably figured I was going to harm it. *"THE SWAN IS SO BEAUTIFUL,"* I thought. "How could anybody hurt her?" I noticed the swan had really big wings like an angel, so *I DECIDED TO NAME HER ANGIE,* which is Latin for "angel."

After a while Angie started to warm up to me, as she knew that I was not going to harm her. She looked out the window and watched all the trees and the sky go by, just like you would do when you go for a car ride. After all, it was Angie's first ride in a vehicle.

Angie was so fascinated by all the sights as I drove past the mountains and lakes of the Yukon Territory. I bet she was thinking to herself, "now traveling in your truck is not my bird's-eye view, but still, *TRAVELING THIS WAY IS A LOT EASIER THAN HAVING TO FLAP MY WINGS ALL DAY!*"

Just before reaching my home in Whitehorse Yukon; Angie became quite brave by coming close to me and making soft swan calls. I think ANGIE WAS TRYING TO TELL ME SOMETHING.

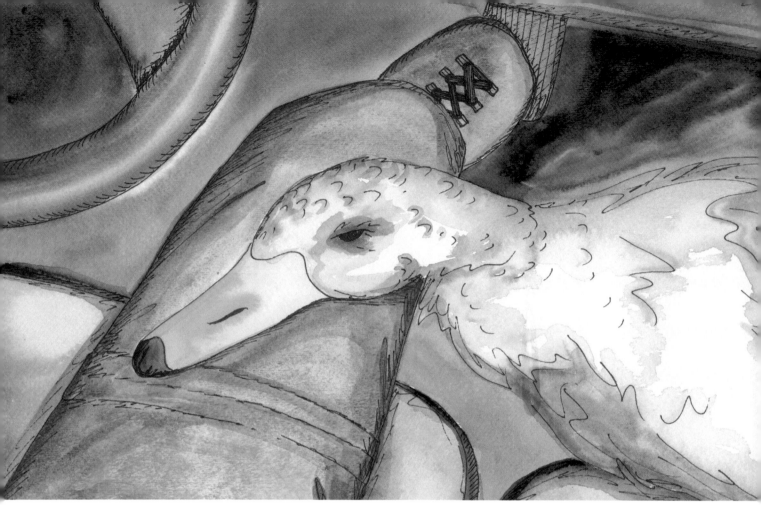

Angie rested her beak and head on my leg. I think she was saying, "Hey there, thanks for rescuing me from the side of the road. *I THINK YOU'RE GREAT AND I WANT TO BE YOUR FRIEND.*"

When I brought Angie into my home, she was a little nervous at first. I broke up some lettuce and soaked it in a big bowl of water for her to eat. She started gobbling it all down. She then *MADE HERSELF RIGHT AT HOME* and started walking around *EXPLORING HER NEW SURROUNDINGS.* I soon discovered that Angie did a lot of poo-poo after she ate, and I had to be very careful not to step on the poo-poo!

The next day I brought Angie to the local veterinarian. The vet examined Angie and told me that she had a very bruised wing, but *LUCKILY HER WING WASN'T BROKEN.* She bandaged Angie's wing very carefully and told me that it would take approximately two weeks before Angie would be able to fly again. I thought about this for a while. Did I really want Angie to fly away? I would probably never see her again if she flew away. This made me feel kind of sad.

After we got home from the vet, I placed Angie in the goldfish pond I have near my home. **ANGIE WAS THRILLED** that I had placed aquatic plants in there for her to eat. She also liked the fountain that sprayed water up in the air. Each day for the next two weeks I placed Angie in the pond. The exercise she got swimming around in the water was also good for her rehabilitation.

CACACACAACAA

After Angie ate her meals each day and finished swimming in the pond, she would start making swan calls for me to come and play with her. She made a sound like, "*CAAAAA CACAAAAA-CACAAAA.*" It was very loud!

After a while, I didn't mind Angie's loud sounds. I started imitating Angie's calls and she walked up really close to me. I got down on my knees at Angie's eye level, and *WE BEGAN SQUAWKING TO EACH OTHER* like two swans having a conversation. I'm not sure of what was being said in swan language, but *WE BOTH WERE SURE HAVING LOTS OF FUN!*

Each night when it was time to go to sleep, Angie followed me to my bedroom. I laid a nice fluffy pillow on the floor for her to lie on beside my bed. *I GENTLY STROKED HER HEAD, WHICH SHE REALLY LIKED.*

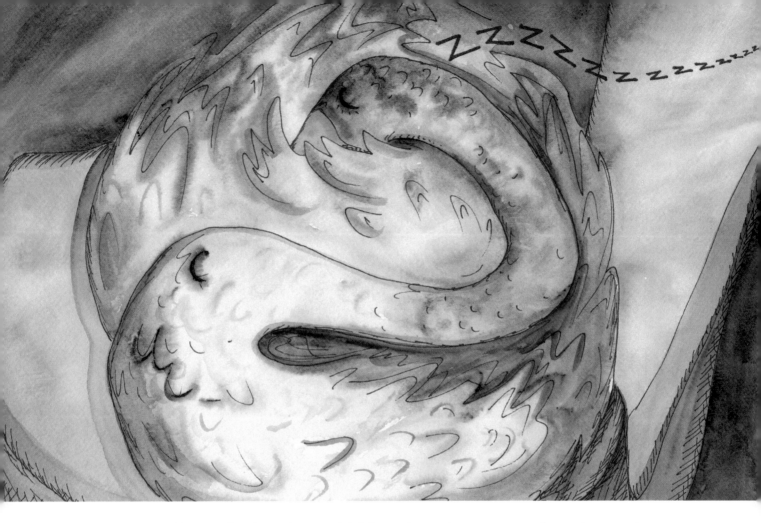

Angie would immediately curl up and fall fast asleep. She was so cute lying down with her head and neck tucked away in her feathery body. As I looked at her, I thought to myself, "I would like to keep Angie as a pet forever. *I DO NOT WANT HER TO FLY AWAY — EVER!* If she did fly away, I would never see her again."

After having Angie around my home for the past week or so, *I BECAME CURIOUS ABOUT TUNDRA SWANS* and how they live in the wild. I did some research on the internet and found out some interesting facts about these magnificent birds.

I found that tundra swans mate for life and pair up for nearly an entire year before breeding. They breed as pairs spread out across the Arctic tundra at the top of North America. *IN THE YUKON, THIS AREA IS KNOWN AS THE NORTH SLOPE.*

I also discovered that in the winter, tundra swans live along the Pacific coast, from British Columbia to as far south as California.

The tundra swan builds nests made out of large stick dwellings lined with moss and grasses. The nests are usually situated close to a pond or other water sources. During the breeding season the tundra swan sleeps almost entirely on land, but in the winter, it sleeps more often on water.

Females incubate 3 to 5 eggs for 32 days while the males guard the nest. Then after a month, *THE EGGS BREAK OPEN AND BABY SWANS ARE BORN.*

After reading all these fascinating facts about tundra swans, I had second thoughts about keeping Angie as a pet. If I kept her she would be missing out on meeting a mate. She would not be able to have little baby swans and fly long distances to and from her winter and summer homes. *I WAS UNSURE OF WHAT I SHOULD DO WITH ANGIE.*

After two weeks, I removed the bandage from Angie's wing. ANGIE WAS INSTANTLY DELIGHTED as she began to sing and flap her angelic wings ever so gracefully and squawk ever so happily. HER WING WAS FINALLY HEALED!

It was a glorious sunny morning with the sun rising over the mountains. Angie went to the big window in our living room, stared out at the sky and watched as some birds flew by. After Angie saw the birds she turned and looked at me, squawking softly and looking a little sad. "WHAT WAS SHE THINKING," I wondered.

I thought maybe Angie was telling me that she was ready to go back to her natural habitat. *SHE WAS FINALLY FEELING HEALTHY AGAIN* and wanted to go explore the land of endless ponds, mountains, trees and skies. But would this mean our close friendship would be over? Would I ever see my beloved swan again?

Nevertheless, I picked Angie up and brought her to my truck. *I WAS GOING TO SET HER FREE!*

After a short drive, I carried Angie to the McIntyre Marsh, a nearby wetland that attracts all kinds of waterfowl, such as ducks, geese, and swans. *I KNEW THIS WAS GOING TO BE HARD FOR ME TO DO.*

I gently put Angie on the water, and she immediately started paddling with her big webbed feet up the stream. I yelled out, "GOODBYE, ANGIE, IT WAS A PLEASURE KNOWING YOU!"

It was kind of sad to be saying goodbye to Angie, but I knew it was the right thing to do.

I waited a short while then drove up a big hill overlooking the wetland where I released Angie. I made a big swan call, "CAACAAAAA-CAAACAAAAAA".

I saw Angie get out of the water and onto a nearby bank. Angie looked in my direction and returned my call several times. Angie would not leave the bank; she kept calling out to me. "FLY AWAY, ANGIE," I SAID. "YOU NEED TO FLY SOUTH AND MEET UP WITH ALL THE OTHER SWANS BEFORE IT GETS TOO COLD." I finally drove away in my truck, hoping that she would get my message. I felt a teardrop on my cheek.

Angie eventually flew south. The following spring a large flock of swans flew near my home near Golden Horn Mountain. One of the swans left the flock for a few minutes and swooped down very low over my head, *SQUAWKING VERY LOUDLY AS IF TO SAY "HELLO, HELLO!"* I am sure that it was Angie, although her feathers looked pure white.

I never saw Angie again and I always wonder how she is doing today.

THE REAL ANGIE

In the fall when I found Angie by the side of the road, she was a juvenile swan, meaning she had not fully matured to an adult yet.

During the time that I was helping Angie get better to the time I set her free, Angie's feathers were mostly silvery gray and, she had a pinkish, mottled bill with a black tip.

Bewick's Swan, Jan. 2006, Saitama JAPAN. Photo taken by Maga-chan. Licensed under CC BY-SA 2.5 via Wikimedia

Dr. Wayne Lynch, photographer

The photo above is how Angie looks today. After I released Angie, the following winter her bill color gradually turned to black and yellow as she transformed from a juvenile to an adult.

Angie's feathers also began turning white in late December and by mid-March of the following year, they were **PURE WHITE**.

ABOUT THE TUNDRA SWAN

The tundra swan (*Cygnus columbianus*) is a small Holarctic swan, also known as a "whistling swan." Tundra swans weigh between 7.5 and 21 pounds with a wingspan from five to seven feet. They breed on the high tundra, above the Arctic Circle across the top of North America. In the **YUKON**, this area is known as the **NORTH SLOPE**.

SWAN HAVEN

In the springtime, usually April of each year, thousands of trumpeter and tundra swans arrive in the Yukon. Many of these swans come to M'Clintock Bay in Marsh Lake, locally known as Swan Haven. Swan Haven is approximately 40 kilometres south of the city of Whitehorse. Before landing at Swan Haven, these swans can be seen for miles flying as family units in their well-known "V" formations.

The swans are drawn to the open waters of the bay that offer shallow water with an accessible and plentiful supply of aquatic plants (during this time, most adjacent waterways are still frozen). *SWAN HAVEN IS AN IMPORTANT LAYOVER FOR SWANS ON THEIR LONG MIGRATION TO NESTING GROUNDS IN THE ARCTIC.*

These majestic birds are quite an attraction, so much so that a *CELEBRATION OF SWANS,* a premiere bird festival, is held throughout April and early May of each year. Yukoners and people from all around the world travel to Swan Haven to celebrate the arrival of these stunning creatures. The Celebration of Swans event offers fun and education for the whole family with birding tours, bird identification and photography workshops, art exhibits, school programs, storytelling and contests. Staff at the Swan Haven Interpretive Centre help visitors appreciate and identify the two species of swans and also other waterfowl, including widgeons, Canada Geese, Northern Pintails, shorebirds, and eagles. One of the features of the centre is its three dimensional "swans" created by *YUKON CHILDREN.*

 FriesenPress

Suite 300 - 990 Fort St
Victoria, BC, Canada, V8V 3K2
www.friesenpress.com

Copyright © 2015 by Todd Daniel Pilgrim
First Edition — 2015

Cygnus bewickii 01" by Maga-chan - photo taken by Maga-chan. Licensed under
CC BY-SA 2.5 via Wikimedia Commons - http://commons.wikimedia.org
wiki/File:Cygnus_bewickii_01.jpg#/media/File:Cygnus_bewickii_01.jpg.

Illustrations by Juliann Fraser
Illustrator photo by Vanessa Falle

All rights reserved. No part of this publication may be reproduced
in any form, or by any means, electronic or mechanical, including
photocopying, recording, or any information browsing, storage, or
retrieval system, without permission in writing from FriesenPress.

ISBN
978-1-4602-6876-6 (Paperback)
978-1-4602-6877-3 (eBook)

1. Juvenile Nonfiction, Animals

Distributed to the trade by The Ingram Book Company

CPSIA information can be obtained at www.ICGtesting.com
Printed in the USA
BVIW12n0439290915
420054BV00001B/1